DATE DUE

SEP 21 2020
FEB 21 2020

JAN 0 6 2005
2 2004
2004
2004
8 2004
2004
8 2004
2004
2004

MAKE WAY FOR DUMB BUNNIES

Story by Sue Denim · Pictures by Dav Pilkey

THE BLUE SKY PRESS / AN IMPRINT OF SCHOLASTIC INC. NEW YORK

To my loving husband,
Rev. Darryl F. Denim S. D.

For Kevin Lewis D. P.

THE BLUE SKY PRESS

For information regarding permission, please write to:
Permission Department,
The Blue Sky Press, an imprint of Scholastic Inc.,
555 Broadway, New York, NY 10012.

The Blue Sky Press is a trademark of Scholastic Inc.

Library of Congress Cataloging-in-Publication Data
Denim, Sue, 1966–
Make way for Dumb Bunnies / story by Sue Denim;
pictures by Dav Pilkey.   p.   cm.
Summary: The Dumb Bunnies have a very active day,
during which they do many things backwards or wrong.
ISBN 0-590-58286-0
[1. Rabbits—Fiction.   2. Humorous stories.]
I. Pilkey, Dav, 1966– ill. II. Title.
PZ7.D4149Mak 1996 [E]—dc20 95-15311 CIP   AC

12 11 10 9 8 7 6 5 4 3 2   8 9/9 0/0
Printed in Singapore   46
First printing, February 1996
The illustrations in this book were done with watercolors,
India ink, acrylics, gouache, skim milk, and Vick's Vap-O-Rub.
Production supervision by Angela Biola

Early one morning, the Dumb Bunnies were spending some quality time apart.

Poppa Bunny was watching the Super Bowl,

Momma Bunny was watching the Orange Bowl...

...and Baby Bunny was watching the Toilet Bowl.

"That's my boy!" said Poppa Bunny.

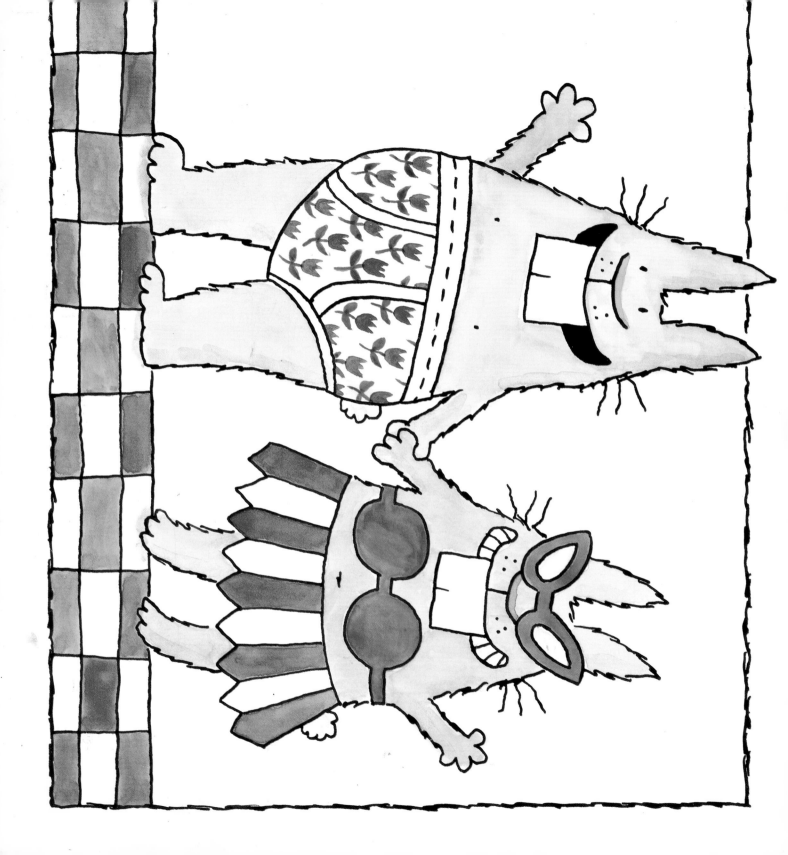

Soon it started to rain. Dark clouds rolled in, and thunder flashed brightly all around.

"It looks like a *perfect* day to go to the beach," said Poppa Bunny.

So they packed three sack lunches...

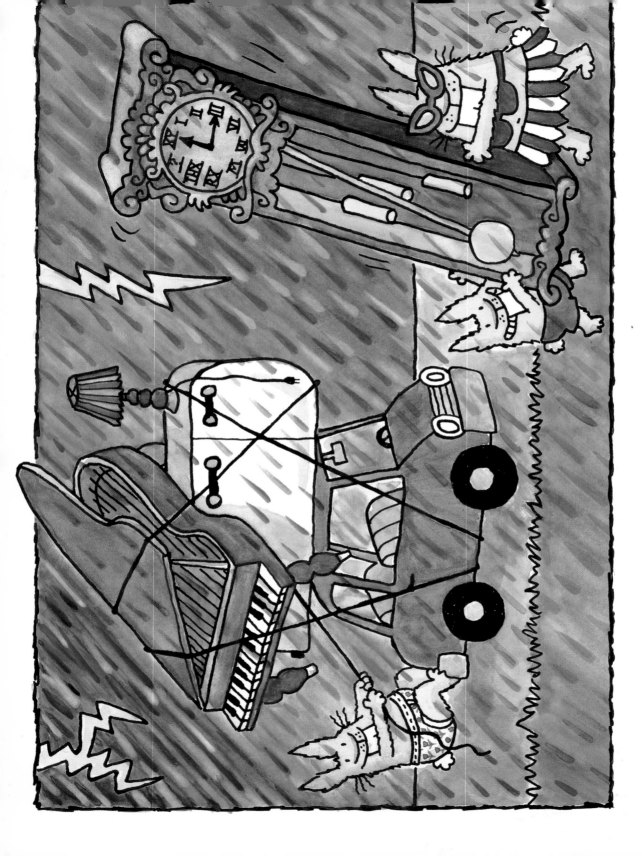

...loaded up the car with everything they needed,

and headed off for the beach.

When they got to the beach, the Dumb Bunnies went in for a swim.

Baby Bunny took his umbrella, because
he didn't want to get wet.

Afterwards, Momma Bunny combed the beach,

Poppa Bunny went fishing in a boat…

...and Baby Bunny blew up an inflatable raft.

"That's my boy!" said Poppa Bunny.

Soon the rain stopped, and the sun came out.
"Looks like bad weather," said Momma Bunny.
So the Dumb Bunnies headed back to town.

On their way, they came across the deal of the century!

"Duh, look!" said Poppa Bunny. "A free car! Let's take it!"

So they did.

When the Dumb Bunnies got to town, they parked their new car and went to see a movie.

Inside the lobby, they bought a tub of popcorn.

But the Dumb Bunnies didn't enjoy the movie very much.

"The screen is too small," said Poppa Bunny.
"And it's too *bright*," said Momma Bunny.

After the movie, the Dumb Bunnies could hardly see a thing.

They looked all over for their new car.
"Duh, I think I found it," said Poppa Bunny.
So they all climbed in and drove toward home.

It was a very bumpy ride.

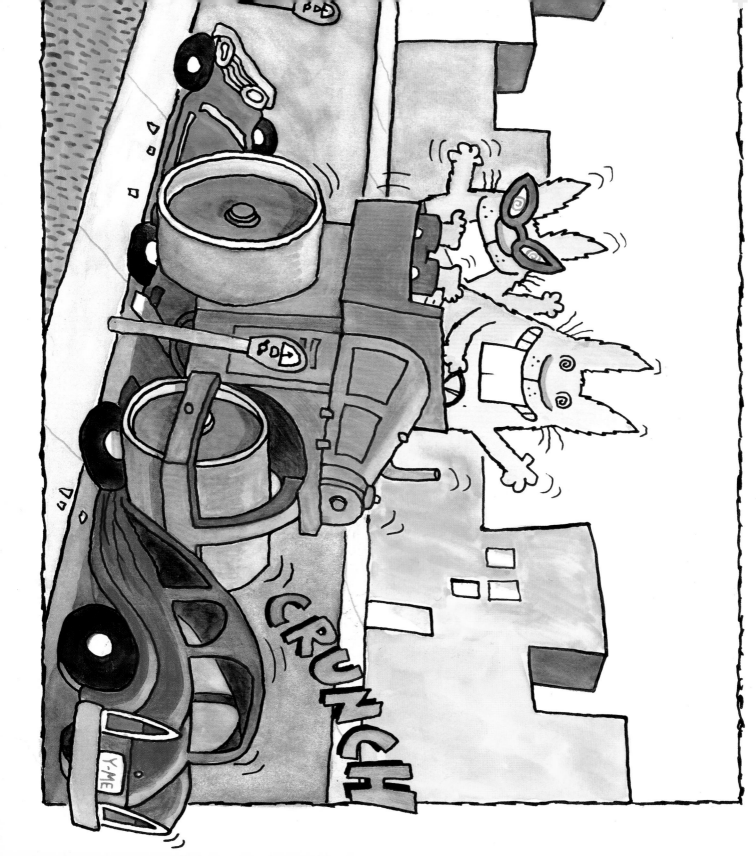

At last, the Dumb Bunnies arrived home safe and sound.

It was getting late and was almost time for bed.

"Can I watch TV in my pajamas?" asked Baby Bunny.

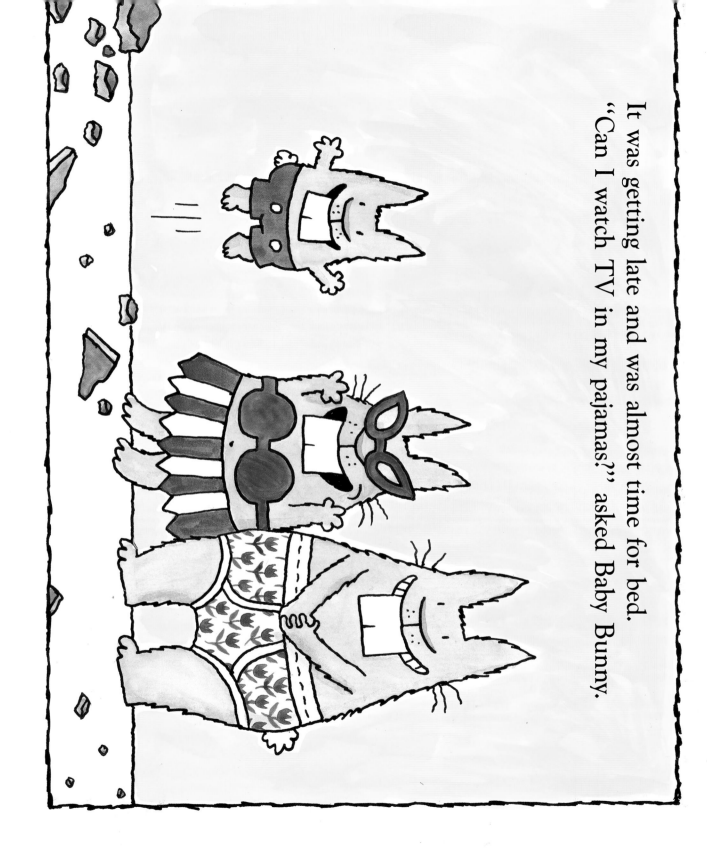

"Dokey-Okey," said Momma and Poppa Bunny.

So Baby Bunny put the TV in his pajamas and watched it all night long.

"That's my boy," said Poppa Bunny.